GREEN DIESEL ERA

DEREK HUNTRISS

Rails

Introduction

In 1955, BR announced its Modernisation Plan with projected costs of £1,240 million to be spread over 15 years, a figure which in the event was greatly exceeded. A key aspect of this plan was the intention to abandon steam traction, the announcement, however, coinciding with the continuing production of Class 9F 2-10-0s.

Instead of introducing well proven standard designs of American construction, BR considered it to be politically preferable to place the Pilot Scheme orders with British manufacturers. This decision is now widely regarded as a serious misjudgement incurring unnecessarily heavy costs for the British taxpayer. The 1955 plan provided for the introduction of 2,500 locos with initial orders for 171 machines. In 1956, for the first time, more diesel locos were built than steam. Several of the Pilot Scheme orders were for batches of 10 or 20 locomotives, forsaking the construction of a prototype, a mistake which BR later came to regret.

Maintenance of these early engines presented a major problem, most locomotives having to share outdated and unsuitable facilities with steam. This problem was addressed by the construction of purpose-built diesel maintenance depots, the first of these being in north London at Devons Road. Most coaching stock was then not equipped for electrical train heating, so many diesel locomotives were fitted with train heating boilers, which often took their weight over the specified axle loading and restricted their route availability. Other weight problems with the early designs became apparent when working loose coupled freight, runaways occurring because of inadequate braking power, this problem being remedied by the building of specially constructed brake tenders which remained in use pending the disappearance of loose coupled freight working.

Prior to the introduction of a standard traction plan for the whole of BR, the Western Region pursued its own policy of introducing diesel hydraulic locomotives, copying the best of available German technology. However, once the standardisation policies were conceived in the mid-1960s, the hydraulics were the first casualties of the diesel era.

With hindsight, BR would have benefited from the evolution of standard types from its pilot scheme designs. As it was, its policies resulted in a wide variety of non-standard types of varying quality, and much time, effort and money was wasted. However, to the enthusiast, the transition from steam was fascinating, with a number of diesel classes appearing and disappearing within a short span of years. Experiments with liveries, too, provided colourful contrasts with the grime and matt black of the ageing steam fleet.

In this title all of the major first generation diesel locomotive types are featured, together with a number of early diesel multiple units (DMUs) and shunters.

Pioneering prototypes and one-off experimental locos have been omitted, most images of these machines having seen publication elsewhere.

Derek Huntriss
Coventry   *March 2014*

Contents

English Electric Co 1,000hp Bo-Bo Type A (1)

Still wearing a coat of primer English Electric Co Bo-Bo Type 1 No D8013 is being pushed off the traverser at Crewe Works by Class 08 shunter No D3802 in this picture taken on 30 August 1964. On the right with dome cover removed can be seen BR Standard Class 2 2-6-2T No 84025. The first twenty of this class were allocated to Devons Road depot in Bow, London to work cross-London transfer freights with the next eight locos allocated to Hornsey depot. After a trial with D8006, D8028–D8034 were allocated for work in highland Scotland, and had tablet catcher recesses built into the cabsides. D8035–D8044 were originally to be allocated to Norwich, but were actually used for empty coaching stock (ECS) workings in and out of London Euston. D8050–D8069 were allocated to the new Tinsley TMD in Sheffield, from where they regularly worked into Lincolnshire and Humberside. D8070–D8127 were sent to operate in the Scottish lowlands. This completed the original orders for 128 locos. With the subsequent order for a further 100 locos, deliveries recommenced with D8128 in January 1966. Tests in 1967 using D8179 and D8317 resulted in locos from D8316 being delivered from the manufacturer with the new electronic control system for working merry-go-round coal trains. *W. Potter/Kidderminster Railway Museum*

Becoming Class 20 No 20123, D8123 was built for English Electric at the Robert Stephenson and Hawthorn works, Darlington. It entered traffic in March 1962 and was allocated to Glasgow's Polmadie (66A) MPD for Scottish lowlands coalfield duties. It was to remain in Scotland for the next twenty-four years, transferring to Eastfield when Polmadie closed in the late 1960s and then Motherwell in the early 1980s. Its final transfer was in 1986 when it left Scotland for Bescot. However its stay at Bescot was brief as it was withdrawn in April 1987. Of all the locomotives delivered under BR's pilot schemes, the D8000 class has outlived most of its contemporaries. The success of these 1,000hp Bo-Bo's lay with the design which incorporated well-proven equipment. Considerable effort was also made to produce an attractive piece of industrial design. With a service availability approaching 90%, the class had the acclaim of their drivers and maintenance men alike. A total of 26 Class 20 locomotives are preserved, including the first of the class built, D8000, which is part of the National Railway Collection at the National Railway Museum in York. The photo was taken in July 1965. *Bill Wright*

English Electric Bo-Bo Type 1 No D8015 at Willesden (1A) mpd on 15 March 1959. Not all of this class were built to the same design, D8000- D8127 being fitted with disc train reporting equipment whilst D8128-D8327 were fitted with four-character route indicators. Of the twenty pilot scheme locos, D8014 was used to conduct signalling tests between Waterloo and Farnborough in order to test AWS equipment installed on certain sections of the South Western section main line. *Both: W. Potter/KRM*

An unidentified English Electric Bo-Bo Type 2 passes through Kensington Olympia with a freight train in May 1967. One problem observed on the run with D8014 described in the previous caption was the poor visibility when running bonnet first. Because of visibility problems with the D8000, D8200 and D8400 classes, BR decided that all future diesel electric locos in this power range would be built to a new Bo-Bo design incorporating two Davey-Paxman engines which were to be placed on each side of a full width driving cab. An initial order for 88 for use on the Scottish Region were placed with the Clayton Equipment Co of Hatton, Derby. By the 1960s all of the old platform buildings at Kensington Olympia had been cleared away and on 24 May 1966 a Motorail terminal opened on the site of the north-west bay platforms with car transport services to Scotland, Wales and the West Country. By 1981 the number of cars using the terminal had dwindled and it closed at the end of the summer season. *J. Fairman/KRM*

Brush Traction Co 1,250/1,365/1,600/2,000hp AIA-AIA Type B(2/3/4)

LEFT In this interesting detailed picture looking south east from the footbridge at March station, Brush A1A-A1A Type 2 No D5522 passes March East Junc signal box with a down freight on 7 October 1968. The up sidings contain a considerable amount of coal traffic in 16-ton unfitted mineral wagons. At this date it could be the start of the sugar beet campaign when factories were building up their stockpiles. Other large industrial users in East Anglia were town gas and cement works. *Bill Wright*

ABOVE Having entered traffic at Sheffield Darnall (41A) mpd only ten days before this picture was taken, Brush Type 2 No D5858 is seen rubbing shoulders with steam locomotives at Blackpool Central mpd on 30 September 1962, having arrived with an excursion. The first member of the class, D5500, had been handed over to the BTC some five years earlier at a ceremony at the Brush Locomotive Works. After extensive trials between Loughborough and Chinley it was delivered to the Great Eastern section of the ER, making its first journey in revenue earning service on 13 November 1957 on the 10.36am Liverpool Street to Clacton. *Peter Fitton*

Featured in this picture taken at Parkeston Quay mpd on 9 August 1965 is Brush A1A-A1A Type 2 No D5576, and behind this locomotive is BTH Bo-Bo Type 1 No D8216. Also on shed that day was Departmental No 27 (formerly Class B1 4-6-0 No 61105) which was still in use for carriage heating purposes. No 61105 remained at Parkeston Quay until approximately July 1966 when it was moved to King's yard in Norwich where it was scrapped shortly afterwards. The depot at Parkeston Quay was situated at the south end of Harwich Parkeston Quay station on the east side of the line. It was a brick built four track dead-ended straight shed with a twin gable style slate roof. Its facilities included a 50ft turntable and a coal stage and in 1947 a brick built one-track straight through shed with a gable style roof was added along the eastern wall. This shed was used for diesel locomotives only. In 1950 the shed was re-roofed with corrugated asbestos as seen here, and in 1960 it was partially demolished but continued in use as a diesel locomotive depot until final closure came in February 1967. *Neville Simms*

This very pleasing image depicts Brush A1A-A1A Type 2 diesel electric No D5551 as it trundles past milepost 51¾ at Colchester with a short down freight consisting of five Vanfits and a few coal empties on 15 January 1968. On the right of the loco a local pub advertises the once popular 'Double Diamond' beer. It was developed by the brewer Samuel Allsopp & Sons of Burton upon Trent in 1876 as an India Pale Ale. Allsopp merged with Ind Coope in 1935. Bottled Double Diamond began to be advertised heavily from 1946, becoming one of four nationally distributed beers by the 1950s. *Bill Wright*

English Electric Co 2,000hp 1Co-Co1 Type C (4)

Still wearing what could be described as steam issue uniforms the crew of English Electric 1Co-Co1 Type 4 No D224 take over this southbound express at Rugby on 29 March 1965. At that point in time the section from Rugby to Euston had not been energised despite electrical equipment being installed as early as 1963. Careful observers will note that the locomotive's LH horn grill has been fitted the wrong way round. Obscured from view behind the loco are the Rugby carriage sheds, in front of which is stabled a Stanier 'Porthole' carriage. Just visible above this carriage is the locomotive shed.

Early footplate tales of when the electrics took over services out of Euston, on what were essentially steam timings slightly accelerated, tell of routinely waiting in Rugby 20min for right time; gaining 20 minutes in the space of 82 miles! Built at the Vulcan Foundry in Newton-le-Willows, No D224 was allocated to Liverpool Edge Hill (8A) when this picture was taken, having been named *Lucania* at Crewe Works on 15 October 1962.
Bill Wright

Looking south from Farington Junction towards Leyland on 24 June 1968, split headcode EE Type 4 No D333 is crossing from down slow to down fast with 4L38, an additional (short term planning or control special) fitted freight. In the distance the careful eye will see a Birmingham Railway Carriage & Wagon Co three car dmu approaching Leyland station. The dilapidated siding on the right is the once-busy entrance to the Leyland Motor Works. In times past trainloads of vehicles were once transported by rail. This works also built Centurion tanks and in the late 1950s and early 1960s it was not uncommon to see trainloads of tanks leaving this siding. The 200-strong fleet took four years to build and entered service with significant front end design differences. The first 125 locomotives, numbers D200 – D324, were all constructed with white marker disc headcodes but British Railways later adapted a new policy of train headcodes displaying a four character train reporting number. Nos. D325 – D344 were built with split headcode boxes displaying two characters either side of the gangway doors. Another policy change meant locomotives were no longer built with gangway doors. As a result, the final batch, Nos. D345 – D399, were all constructed with four character centre headcode panels and without gangway doors, creating a much neater appearance to the front end design. Later, seven of the original Scottish based locomotives (Nos. D260 – D266) were all modified to centre headcode design. *Bill Wright*

ABOVE On 5 March 1967, the last day of through passenger services between Paddington and Birkenhead, EE Type 4 No D297 is recorded with an up working at Capenhurst between Birkenhead and Chester. Problems with the safety of permanent way staff led to all BR diesel locos having the cab fronts or nose-end fronts painted in half warning yellow, to help make approaching trains more visible. The last batch of EE Type 4's were duly delivered already painted in this scheme, while others were treated during works visits or on depots. By the late 1960s the yellow 'warning panels' began to be extended to cover the full nose ends, improving visibility further. *Peter Fitton*

BELOW A classic view of EE Type 4 No D322 as it heads the up 'Caledonian' alongside the recently opened M1 motorway near Welton, south of Rugby, on 6 June 1962. No D322 was the first member of the class to be withdrawn, in 1967, following a severe accident one year earlier on 14 May 1966. Both crew members lost their lives in the cab when several hopper wagons loaded with soda ash broke away from a preceding train on the incline at Moore, south of Warrington. D322 was hauling the 20.40 Euston to Stranraer boat train. Rugby and Edge Hill cranes assisted in clearing the wreckage and D322 was removed to Crewe. *Peter Fitton*

EE Type 4 No D217 *Carinthia* heads a Euston to Glasgow express near Hest Bank on 28 July 1967, the loco receiving the name without ceremony on 16 June 1962. Twenty-five locomotives of this class were named, all after ocean liners and passenger ships. Only the first three were named at a public naming ceremony the others receiving their names at works overhauls between 1960 and 1963. The Cunard liner *Carinthia* had left Liverpool on her maiden voyage on 27 June 1956 with over 800 passengers to Montreal. The *Carinthia* remained on her designed route from Liverpool and Greenock to Quebec and Montreal all her working life in the Cunard fleet. The EE Type 4s fought a rearguard action on the West Coast main line to Euston in the face of advancing electrification and towards the end of their careers saw little all-year round passenger work. *Peter Fitton*

British Thomson-Houston 800hp Bo-Bo Type A(1)

BTH Bo-Bo Type 1 No D8203 bathes in winter sunshine outside Colchester Diesel Depot on 15 January 1968. Most duties for this class of locomotives were confined to the areas served by Stratford, Ipswich and Finsbury Park depots. Primarily intended for use on main line and cross-country freight working, No D8200 and its nine pilot scheme sisters were initially allocated to Devons Road Depot. Having travelled from the builders, Yorkshire Engine Company, the British Transport Commission (BTC) received D8200 at a ceremony at Euston station on 18 November 1957. All ten members of the initial order were subjected to extensive trials over the Settle & Carlisle route prior to delivery, most workings with eleven coaches from Sheffield Wincobank down sidings to Appleby and return. With the decline of London freight duties in the late 1960s the fleet of 44 locos found themselves redundant, withdrawals taking place between 1969 and 1971, the last members of the class being withdrawn from traffic on 27th March 1971. However, four of the Class, D8203/33/37 and D8243, escaped scrapping and were taken into Departmental stock for carriage heating duties. These duties lasted for around ten years at a wide range of locations from Swansea to Dundee. *Bill Wright*

This picture of BTH Bo-Bo Type 1 No D8241 taken at Doncaster station on 20 March 1968 could be a record of one of its last movements in traffic before withdrawal on 14 April. It is possible that the loco was visiting 'The Plant' for assessment as a carriage heating unit. These were moved to BREL Doncaster for removal of non-essential equipment and were renumbered ADB968000-3. However, when relocated to East Anglia for the transition to electrically heated stock it was discovered that the long period without works attention had taken its toll. Colchester depot undertook some work on the locomotives, but the intended work was covered by newer locomotives. D8233 and the other two locomotives were regarded as surplus to requirements. D8233 was transferred to Healey Mills depot for storage alongside other redundant locomotives; from here it was purchased for preservation in 1984. *Bill Wright*

British Thomson-Houston Bo-Bo Type 1 No D8202 is seen in profile in this picture taken at Willesden (1A) mpd on 15 March 1959. Following the headlong plunge into quantity production of diesel locomotives when BR's Pilot Scheme was abandoned, British Thomson-Houston Co received orders for an additional thirty four of the BTH Type 1 design, of which ten pilot scheme locos had already been produced. These locos carried the same Paxman 16YHXL diesel engine as had been fitted to the North British Loco Co pilot scheme Type 1 (The D8400 class), although it would appear to have been seen as a marginally better design than the latter, which received no follow-on orders. The Paxman power unit was the chief cause of failure with this type, being officially described as 'unsatisfactory and dirty', with the engine suffering piston seizures and requiring excessive maintenance. In an attempt to get the best out of the D8200 and D8400 classes they were all allocated to one region – the ER – this involving transferring some of the D8200s from the LMR. The BTH/Clayton version seems to have been preferred for station pilot and empty stock work.
W. Potter/KRM

A number of Type 1 Bo-Bo diesels stand outside Stratford diesel depot on 3 June 1967. They include British Thomson-Houston Bo-Bo Type 1 number D8212 which heads a line of four, of which the inner two are NBL type 1s. There was a delay of almost one year between the delivery of the last pilot scheme loco, No D8209, and the first of the production versions, D8210. This must have been due to restrictions in manufacturing resources as the production version was, except for a later 'mark' of traction motor, identical in all respects. No D8210 was completed in October 1958, the last of the batch D8243, being delivered by Clayton in February 1961. BR policies eventually affected the future of this class, wagon-load freight proving increasingly uneconomical. This, coupled with the fact they could not be employed on passenger work in the winter months, led to their early withdrawal. *W. Potter/KRM*

North British Loco Co 800hp Bo-Bo Type A(1)

North British/GEC Type A (later Type 1) No D8408 stands at Stratford shed in company with D8200 class units on 3 June 1967. All ten locomotives in this class were allocated to Stratford motive power depot where they were used on freight traffic, including inter-regional workings to Hither Green and New Cross Gate, in addition to working parcels traffic between Liverpool Street and Southend. They closely resembled the stark appearance of the pioneer LMSR Bo-Bo No 10800 which NBL had built in 1950. Outwardly they were box-like and austere although some effort had been made to improve the design of the cab by placing the doors in the side of the cab instead of at the ends. Sensibly, no production orders of the class were ordered, all being withdrawn by 1968. *W. Potter/KRM*

Newly delivered North British Loco Co Type 1 No D8401 is awaiting acceptance trials at Doncaster Works on 13 July 1958. While the D8200 Class suffered problems with the Paxman engines, these were worse on the D8400s because inadequate ventilation resulted in frequent engine seizures. They were fitted with a non-standard type of electro-magnetic control equipment (coded 'red circle' by BR) which was prone to failure, and they could not operate in multiple with locomotives fitted with the more common electro-pneumatic ('blue star') controls. Stratford depot did its best to keep these locomotives in traffic but when engine room fires occurred they seriously disrupted traffic. Being non-standard and unreliable, the locomotives were an obvious candidate for early withdrawal. After somewhat unglamorous and chequered careers on the ER they were withdrawn between February and September 1968. Apart from No D8404, which was sold to Cox and Danks of North Acton in June 1968, the class was stored at Stratford until February 1969 when they were moved down the Midland main line to the yard of G. Cohen Ltd at Kettering where they were scrapped. *W. Potter/KRM*

Metropolitan-Vickers 1,200hp Co-Bo Type B (2)

Metropolitan-Vickers Co-Bo Type 2 No D5717 is seen in its original condition at Cricklewood (14A) mpd on 4 October 1959 – wraparound cab windows and no yellow panels. Becoming BR Class 28, Metropolitan-Vickers Type 2 diesel locomotives, or 'Metrovicks' as they were popularly known, they were built as part of the British Railways 1955 Modernisation Plan. The locos had a Co-Bo wheel arrangement (a 6-wheel bogie at one end, a 4-wheel bogie at the other) – unique in British Railways practice though not uncommon in other countries, notably Japan. This affected their route availability, due to the different axle loading at each end of the loco, and made maintenance more complicated. Almost from the beginning the Metrovick's Crossley engines were problematic. They suffered frequent failures and by 1961 the entire class was handed back to the manufacturer for remedial work on the engines and to cure problems with cab windows falling out while running. The cab windows were modified such that instead of wrapping round to the side, the outer front windows were replaced by a flat piece of glass to the front only.
W. Potter/ KRM

TOP Photographed near Morecambe South Jct 'Metrovick' Co-Bo Type 2 No D5705 heads a Lancaster to Barrow service on 29 August 1964. By this time its original wraparound windows had been replaced with smaller panes of glass and yellow warning panels had been applied. As in the case of the Brush Traction A1A-A1A layout, the extra wheels did not offer any real power advantage over the Bo-Bo arrangement.

BOTTOM Another Summer Saturday August 1964 'Metrovick' picture. This time an unidentified member of the class is seen arriving with an excursion at Windermere Lakeside station. When the services stopped on the line in 1965, the station fell into disrepair. The station reopened as part of the heritage Lakeside and Haverthwaite Railway in 1973, with trains running to the nearby station of Haverthwaite,
Both: David J. Mitchell

This unidentified 'Metrovick' Co-Bo Type 2 is seen south of Morecambe South Junction with a Barrow to Lancaster working on 29 August 1964. These machines had commenced trial working on 7 July 1958, D5700 taking a fourteen coach test train from Metropolitan-Vickers works at Bowsfield, Stockton, to Leeds. Trouble was experienced and several unscheduled stops had to be made, resulting in a 90 minute late arrival on the return journey. D5700/1 hauled a special test train which consisted of 25 fitted 'Platefits' loaded with 50 containers on 1 October 1958 from Hendon to Gushetfaulds Goods via Leicester, Sheffield, Leeds, Carlisle, Beattock, Carstairs and Motherwell. The inaugural run of the London to Glasgow 'Condor' fitted freight commenced on 16 March 1959, the main attraction to potential customers being that containers were collected in the late afternoon with a guaranteed delivery in Glasgow the following morning for a cost of £16 for a small container and £18 for a large container.
David J. Mitchell

Another view at Morecambe South Junction on 29 August 1964. This time 'Metrovick' Co-Bo Type 2 No D5717 heads a northbound passenger train from Lancaster to Barrow. By November 1959 demand for the 'Condor' service was flagging, some workings consisting of only 13 wagons and one engine. As a result of locomotive problems no fewer than seventeen out of twenty were stopped for repairs at Cricklewood, their dutes on the 'Condor' being performed by Stanier Class 5 4-6-0s. In July 1962 the 'Condor' was back up to its full load, then entrusted to Type 4s, the Co-Bos having been returned to Metropolitan-Vickers. Following this they were relocated to Barrow, ending their days on local passenger and freight duties.
David J. Mitchell

British Railways/Sulzer 1,160/1,250hp Bo-Bo Type B(2)

This pairing of BR Sulzer Class 25 No D7595 and English Electric Type 4 No D328 was captured on the West Coast main line working a down parcels train near Forton, north of Garstang, on 20 June 1970. From No D5151 onwards the Sulzer engine was uprated to 1,250hp, these locos becoming Class 25/0, 25/1, 25/2 or 25/3; the engine seen here is a Class 25/2. On this type the airhorns were located on each side of the rooftop four panel route indicator box and although rarely used the gangway doors were still fitted. Although obscured by the pilot loco, D328 has a four character train reporting number. Nos. D325–D344 were built with 'split' headcode boxes, which displayed two characters either side of the locomotive's central gangway doors. Another policy decision led to the discontinuing of the gangway doors (which enabled train crew to move between two or three locomotives in multiple). The Class 40, as the EE Type 4s were later designated under TOPS, became one of the most successful of the pilot scheme designs, some examples surviving in traffic for over 25 years. *Peter Fitton*

BR Sulzer Type 2 No D7505 sits in the sun at Sandiacre. Unfortunately out of view to the right, a plate wagon situated towards the rear of 87 trip sits on the dirt; hence the appearance of the Toton breakdown vans on the adjacent track. What appears to be a Trent Motor Traction Co Leyland Tiger Cub also sits in the station yard at Stapleford & Sandiacre in this 31 March 1965 picture. Situated on the ex-Midland Railway Erewash Valley main line from Trent to Chesterfield the station at Stapleford & Sandiacre closed to passenger traffic on 2 January 1967. It was the constant output of coal from the many collieries in the North Midlands Area that together with other freight traffic on the North-South axis made the Erewash Valley line so extremely busy. The coal trains were assembled at the great Toton Marshalling Yard, which began immediately south of Stapleford & Sandiacre Station. A Green Party document prepared in November 2009 recommended that the line between Trent Junction and Trowell Junction, then only used by freight traffic, be re-opened for passenger traffic with stations reinstated at Stapleford & Sandiacre and Ilkeston. A proposed £6.5m station in Ilkeston is one of four schemes that successfully applied for money from a £20m Department for Transport fund. Transport Secretary Patrick McLoughlin said the scheme had been awarded £4.5m from the New Station Fund. The station will open in December 2014 and will connect Ilkeston to Northern Rail's Sheffield to Nottingham route. *Bill Wright*

TOP The final development of the BR/Sulzer Bo-Bo Type 2 involved a complete re-design of the bodywork, the air intake grills being positioned in the roof over the engine room and the gangway doors in the front ends being removed. These arrangements were enhanced by the two-tone green livery with a neatly incorporated yellow warning panel. Here No D5244 is captured on 30 March 1964 as it trundles light engine through Derby.

BOTTOM Wearing an experimental orange warning panel No D5159 departs from Tees Yard with a mixed freight on 17 April 1967. This was a Middlesbrough Division Headquarters trial with three locos sporting 'hi-visibility' front ends.
D5153 – Saturn/Yellow panel
D5159 – Yellow/Orange
D5162 – Yellow special fluorescent paint panel. In the train consist are a number of Conflat-A's with demountable containers. *Both: Bill Wright*

In steam days, the maximum load for an unassisted Stanier Class 5 up the 1 in 50 out of Bradford Exchange was seven coaches, anything more than that would have been assisted by a banker, at least as far as Bowling Junction at the top of the gradient. The start out of Exchange was a little easier with the gradient starting beyond the platform end and, usually, the loco that had brought in the empty stock would give the train a push to the end of the platform. Here Leeds Holbeck (55A) depot's BR Sulzer Type 2 No D5251 assists Low Moor (56F) mpd's Stanier Class 5 No 44667 past St Dunstans Junction on 25 July 1967. During November & December 1967 Holbeck Nos D5248 – D5251 were re-allocated to Carlisle Upperby (12B) mpd.
Peter Fitton

BR/Sulzer Bo-Bo Type 2 No D5130 is seen arriving at Perth with a Glasgow to Dundee train on 18 July 1966. The batch of locos Nos D5114–D5132 were fitted with tablet catchers on the side of the drivers cab for use on the Far North Line from Inverness. Also very visible were the roof-mounted headcode boxes fitted from D5114, giving an outward appearance very similar to the later Class 25 but without horn grills. Locos used on the Highland Section of the Scottish Region were also fitted with twin headlights in the centre of the front end with the gangway doors sealed off. The pilot scheme locomotives were delivered in overall green livery with a grey roof and black below the body. D5000 was delivered with a narrow white stripe at waist level while the remainder sported a broad white stripe at solebar level. At first green liveried locos had plain green ends, but this was changed later to small yellow warning panels, and then to full yellow ends, some locos receiving these while still in green livery. At least one loco, D5005, is recorded in 1966 as having two-tone green livery applied along with the small yellow warning panel in a similar manner to Class 47s and some Class 25s. *Bill Wright*

On the former Lancashire & Yorkshire Railway route from Whalley to Blackburn two-tone green liveried BR/Sulzer Type 2 No D5255 (later designated Class 25 No 25105 under TOPS) heads a train of soda ash wagons from Carlisle and is seen at Wilpshire on 20 April 1968. The first two wagons of this type, Nos 4000+4001, were built by Herederos de Ramon Mugica, Irun, Spain in 1966 and were followed by wagons from Pressed Steel the same year. 4000+4001 were to become STS 53400+53401 to design PC 011A as PCW wagons, i.e. vacuum with through air-brakes. The remaining 25 were PCVs to PC 012A. These lasted in traffic until around 1976 when they were replaced by a new batch of 15 air-braked PCAs from Procor Nos PR 9475-9489. D5255 was delivered new to Toton (18A) mpd on 6 March 1964 and during its career it was allocated to three Eastern Region depots and a multitude of depots on the London Midland Region. At the time this photo was taken it was operating from Carlisle Kingmoor (12A) mpd and one month later was transferred to Springs Branch (8F) mpd. *Peter Fitton*

LEFT BR Sulzer Bo-Bo Type 2 No D5277 is seen leaving Peak Forest on 18 April 1967 and will shortly be entering Dove Holes tunnel. The train is 5F68, a Peak Forest to ICI Winnington working, and comprises 18 loaded ICI hoppers of limestone plus brake van. The first diesels used on these services were trialled in 1963. The Midland line north of Matlock was frequently used for testing new diesels fresh out of Derby Works, with fifteen miles of a 1 in 90 ruling grade north of Rowsley. *Bill Wright*

ABOVE An early view of a BR/Sulzer Type 2 taken on 14 May 1959 as No D5004 is depicted outside Eastleigh mpd. The first of the class had arrived on the Southern Region in January 1959 when it was used for crew training. Fifteen of the initial twenty were diverted for use on the Southern Region to cover for delays in delivery of Sulzer Type 3s (later Class 33). Here the weight was too much and the locos in question had to have their boilers removed before they were accepted. *W. Potter/KRM*

Birmingham Railway Carriage & Wagon Co 1,160/1,250hp Bo-Bo Type B(2)

Seen on 4 August 1962 BRCW Bo-Bo Type 2 No D5362 has arrived at Ballachulish and will form the 4.25pm departure to Oban. Modifications to the Scottish Region's engines in this class included a recess for the tablet catcher and sliding cabside windows. This group of locos was later formed into BR Class 26 and Class 27. Whilst there were a number of technical modifications built into the Class 27 they were easily distinguishable by their four character headcode panel, the Class 26 having disc route indicators.
Neville Simms

Birmingham Railway Carriage & Wagon Co Bo-Bo (later type 2) No D5322 stands outside Loch Gorm diesel depot (Inverness) in company with BR/Sulzer Type 2 No D5131 on 29 July 1962. Inverness was the first depot in Scotland to receive any BR/Sulzer Type 2s. Nineteen would be delivered, all from Derby Works, and were used alongside a number of BRCW Type 2s and English Electric Type 1s to oust steam from the Highlands. Although all the Class 24s at Inverness had been built at Derby they would rarely return there for overhaul. The first choice for scheduled heavy repair was the former GNSR workshops at Inverurie, and when this closed they were sent to the workshops at St Rollox, Glasgow. The delivery of the nineteen Derby built Type 2s began with D5114 during the week of 23 April 1960, continuing until September when D5132 reached Inverness. June was the busiest month for deliveries with D5119 – D5123 received.
Neville Simms

A classic line up of steam and diesel motive power captured at Aberdeen Ferryhill (61B) mpd on 17 July 1965. Maintenance of the early diesel locomotives presented a major problem, particularly when they had to share outdated and unsuitable facilities with steam. Here it is interesting to compare the yellow panels on the EE Type 4s Nos D358 (left) and D265 (right). Ferryhill was the location of Aberdeen's first engine shed, situated within the `V' of the junction between the Aberdeen and Deeside Railways. The 1850 engine shed was a modest affair capable of housing two engines under cover and another two partly sheltered from the elements. It was situated on the west side of the main line close to the River Dee. The Ferryhill shed was enlarged following the appointment of Dugald Drummond as Locomotive Superintendent of the Caledonian Railway in 1882, and in response to both his construction of larger engines and the increasing fish traffic at the period. The first diesel locomotives arrived in 1958, displacing steam locomotives used for shunting. Main-line diesel locomotives soon followed, and complete dieselisation was achieved in 1966.
Bill Wright

Birmingham Railway Carriage & Wagon Co Bo-Bo Type 2s No D5325 and D5332 head the 5pm departure from Wick to Inverness (due 9.56pm) on 6 September 1961. The train which consisted of four coaches included a full buffet car and a Braked Gangway (BG) vehicle had been added. This was strengthened at Georgemas Junction with two more coaches and BG from Thurso making a total of eight bogies going forward from Georgemas Junction. The train maintained good time all the way to Dingwall, D5325 being detached at Helmsdale, but at Conon the single line tablet was dropped causing a seventeen minute delay. The Inverness based examples of this class were particularly associated with the Far North Line and Kyle of Lochalsh Line, as well as operating south of Inverness on the Highland Main Line. One notable duty, shared with locally based Class 24s, was to operate 'The Royal Highlander' Inverness to London Euston sleeping car express as far south as Perth, a demanding turn which sometimes required three locomotives working in multiple. The availability of surplus Class 37 and 47 locomotives in the late 1970s and early 1980s displaced the Class 26s from passenger workings and from most goods traffic north of Inverness.
John Langford

British Railways/Sulzer 'Peaks' 2,300/2,500hp 1Co-Co1 Type C(4)

BR/Sulzer/Brush/ Type 4 1Co-Co1 No D188 is ready to head north from Leeds City over the Settle & Carlisle route with the St Pancras to Glasgow 'Thames Clyde Express' on 29 August 1967. In 1962, the 'Thames Clyde' took eight hours and 50 minutes for the complete journey, leaving London at 10.15 and then calling first at Leicester London Road at 11.52. Further stops were made at Trent and Chesterfield before reaching Sheffield Midland station at 13.19 and Leeds City at 14.25 – so this latter stage of 39 miles took over an hour as a result of subsidence-induced speed restrictions. From here the train ran non-stop to Carlisle (arrival 16.38). Three more stops were made at Annan, Dumfries and Kilmarnock before reaching Glasgow St Enoch at 19.05. The rival 'Royal Scot' on the West Coast route stopped only twice and took seven hours, twenty minutes. However the 'Thames Clyde' provided a useful service from the East Midlands and Yorkshire to Scotland. The train lost its title in May 1974 when the West Coast Main Line was electrified to Glasgow, but the service continued to run until 1976. *Bill Wright*

BR/Sulzer 'Peak' 1Co-Co1 No D111 is seen south of Preston at Farington Junction with 1M31, the SO 14:10 Blackpool to Nottingham Midland on 17 June 1963. In the course of its journey this train travelled over a number of unusual lines. The first was the Wigan (NW) Avoiding line (the Whelley Loop). This 5m 26ch line was built by the Lancashire Union Railway in 1869 bypassing Wigan to the east and being used mainly for freight. Stations on this line were opened at Whelley and Amberswood but for only three months between 1 January and 1 March 1872. The line survived until 1976. The next unusual part of its journey was the 37ch between Cheadle North Jct and Cheadle Jct, finally traversing the 19ch between Dore & Totley West Jct and Dore & Totley South Jct.

P. Hutchinson / Manchester Locomotive Society Collection

British Railways/Sulzer 'Peak' 1Co-Co1 Type 4 (later Class 45/0) No D76 comes off the Settle & Carlisle route at Settle Junction with an up freight on 12 March 1966. The 1963 Beeching Report into the restructuring of British Rail recommended the withdrawal of all passenger services from the Settle & Carlisle line. Some smaller stations had closed in the 1950s. In May 1970 all stations except for Settle and Appleby West were closed, and its passenger service cut to two trains a day in each direction, leaving mostly freight. Few express passenger services continued to operate: the 'Waverley' from London St Pancras to Edinburgh Waverley via Nottingham ended in 1968 while the 'Thames-Clyde Express' from London to Glasgow Central via Leicester lasted until 1976. Night sleepers from London to Glasgow continued until 1976. After that a residual service from Glasgow – cut back at Nottingham (three trains each way) – survived until May 1982. *David J. Mitchell*

On the Midland lines out of St Pancras, the 'Peak' BR/Sulzer Type 4s were concentrated on all main line trains. A comprehensive, regular interval timetable was introduced with interconnecting trains for Sheffield hourly, alternately via Derby or Nottingham, with semi-fast trains feeding into each at Leicester. The 'Peaks' reliably achieved running speeds of 90mph and were equally at home on freight workings although the heavy Toton to Brent coal workings were usually entrusted to pairs of Type 2s. With luggage handling equipment in evidence on the platforms this Midland line scene was taken on 31 March 1965 and depicts Brush/Sulzer/Crompton Type 4 1Co-Co1 No D52 *The Lancashire Fusilier* as it heads the 11:51 Bradford to St Pancras express through Stapleford. *Bill Wright*

TOP BR/Sulzer 'Peak' No D146 is captured leaving Gloucester Eastgate on 19th January 1967. Eastgate station closed on 1 December 1975. This was partly an attempt by BR to cut maintenance costs and partly pressure from local councillors who wanted to rid Gloucester of four of its level crossings.

BOTTOM BR/Sulzer 'Peak' No D23 is seen passing Cleeve signal box, Stoke Orchard, with a parcels train on 3 September 1966. This was the site of Cleeve station, so called to avoid confusion with Bishops Cleeve station on the nearby former GWR Cheltenham to Stratford line.
Both: W. Potter/KRM

An unidentified BR/Sulzer 'Peak' 1Co-Co1 Type 4 heads a passenger working for Bradford Forster Square past the closed station at Bradford Manningham in 1966. Behind the station is Bradford Manningham (55F) mpd. The station was closed under the Beeching Axe on 20 March 1965; unlike the next station on the line, Frizinghall, it has not reopened. In the 1950s, and up to closure in 1965, the Bradford Railway Circle used a hut on the platform at Manningham station for its meetings. In January 2008, it was revealed that the City of Bradford prepared a bid to the Regional Transport Board for £10 million which, combined with the £10 million the council received from the sale of Leeds Bradford Airport, would provide funding for the reopening of Manningham station, as well as a number of other road infrastructure projects in the Aire Valley. *David J. Mitchell*

North British Loco Co 1,000hp/1,100hp Bo-Bo Type B(2)

Once the later engines of this class entered service all the NBL 1,000hp Type 2s were allocated to the Scottish Region, but in their early days the pilot scheme engines were used on London area GN suburban duties. Here an unidentified member of the class is captured in a busy scene at Moorgate station.

To the left is an unidentified London Transport T-Stock electric multiple unit en route for Watford whilst to the right of it is ex-LMS Fowler Class 3 2-6-2T No 40026. The 'T' stock units were replaced from 1961 by the A60 and A62 Stock, with the final train running on 5 October 1962. *W. Potter/KRM*

In this cameo scene taken at Perth on 18 July 1966 two-tone green liveried NBL Type 2 No D6123 has arrived with a Dundee to Glasgow express. Apart from the removal of the water columns little has changed in this view today although the railway worker having a 'fag' by the brazier would probably be wearing a high visibility orange jacket.

Duties for the ten pilot scheme locos of this class were on suburban trains on Great Northern lines around London. Reallocation saw these Eastern Region locos transferred to depots at Hornsey, Ipswich and Stratford for service on the former Great Eastern and London, Tilbury and Southend lines. Proving unsuccessful on these duties they could be seen sheeted over at Peterborough shed awaiting transfer to Scotland where they were to spend the rest of their working lives. In an attempt to salvage something from these locos in 1963, D6123 was selected as a test locomotive and sent to Davey Paxman's works in Colchester to have a new engine fitted. After D6123 was rebuilt with its Paxman engine, it was put back to work on the Glasgow to Aberdeen services. Due to poor reliability of the remaining locos, a further 19 were rebuilt during 1965 with new power units and reclassified along with D6123 as Class 29. After reallocation to Scotland, various members of the class were prone to pyrotechnic displays, D6129 catching fire on 29 March 1967 whilst working in multiple on the 3.15pm Glasgow Buchanan Street to Dundee at Greenloaning, little above the bogies and frames being left intact. *Bill Wright*

English Electric Co 'Baby Deltics' 1,100hp Bo-Bo Type B (2)

In this picture full of railway atmosphere the photographer gets the thumbs up from the second man on 'Baby Deltic' No D5903 as she comes up light engine through Peterborough on 7 October 1968. The headcode denotes a light engine to Hitchin and in all probability the loco had arrived with an engineers' train or may even have assisted a failure. At that time Kings Cross drivers were still learning on engines of this class, prior to that it was only Hitchin crews that 'knew' them. On 12 February 1962 D5903 worked in multiple with D5905 on a coal train from Whitemoor to Bury St Edmunds. It was planned to allocate the class to the Sheffield area

for use on colliery work, a proposal that was never implemented. Instead the class was transferred to Hornsey, partly eliminating steam traction from suburban passenger and empty stock duties. By late April 1962 the availability of Baby Deltics had reached a low ebb, only two being in traffic. As each engine failed it was withdrawn from traffic and stored, pending return to English Electric where an extensive refurbishing programme was put in hand. Despite the extensive modifications failures continued and the class did not escape BR's rationalisation plan, the last member, D5909, being withdrawn in March 1971. *Bill Wright*

D5903 is featured again, this time in February 1966 as it approaches New Southgate with an up passenger working. After acceptance trials were conducted at Doncaster, the class entered service between April and June 1959. Whilst they were nominally based at Hornsey, at weekends they were usually located at Hitchin engine shed. It had been British Rail's original intention to work the locos across London on the widened lines but the locomotives were found to be too heavy. They were put to work on Kings Cross outer suburban duties such as the Cambridge Buffet Express, as well as services from Kings Cross to Moorgate sub-surface platforms via the 'widened lines' (more recently, part of Thameslink). The locomotives were later banned from Moorgate because of excessive exhaust smoke in the tunnels. Here D5903 wears the rectangular yellow warning panel which was later replaced by the overall yellow as seen in the picture opposite. All except Nos D5901 and D5908 finally found their way to George Cohen's Kettering yard, D5903 being withdrawn in November 1968 and broken up in June 1969. *MLS Collection*

North British Loco Co 2,000 hp A1A-A1A

North British Loco Co A1A-A1A No D602 *Bulldog* awaits departure from Liskeard with an up passenger working. The first member of the class, No D600, commenced trials in Scotland in November 1957 prior to travelling to Swindon on 13 January 1958. By the end of January it had received the name *Active, Warship Class* on one side when it was posed for official photographs to be taken. The initial livery applied to this batch of locos was an overall Brunswick green with a single blue-grey line between the cab doors along the body side. On 17 February 1958, No D600 was employed on a special nine coach demonstration run from Paddington to Bristol when it attained speeds of over 90mph. On the return

journey, one of the two 1,000hp engines failed near Badminton, the remainder of the journey being completed on one engine, with arrival back at Paddington being some nineteen minutes late. After working a special to Newton Abbot on 19 April 1958, No D600 commenced revenue earning service two days later on a double return daily trip between Penzance and Plymouth which included 'The Limited' in both directions. These original Type C diesel-hydraulics were intended for both express passenger and freight, but the lighter weight of the diesel-hydraulics compared to the diesel-electrics rendered them less effective on freight haulage. *Colour-Rail*

This picture taken at Plymouth North Road station on 4 July 1961 sees North British Loco Co A1A-A1A No D603 *Conquest* in a somewhat careworn condition as it awaits departure with a somewhat cleaner rake of chocolate and cream Mark 1 coaches. With the introduction of the D800 class, the A1A-A1As were displaced from their principal duties on the West of England main line and were relegated to work on Cornish china clay traffic. Apart from an initial allocation to Swindon, the class spent the whole of its working life allocated to Plymouth Laira mpd until August 1967 when D601/2/4 were transferred to Landore. Whilst at Landore, these locos also worked from Margam and Pantyffynon where instructors were provided. Due to their unsuitabilty the trio were returned to Laira and in December 1967 placed in store with others of the class. The end came for Nos D600/1 on 22 July 1968 when they were towed to Woodham's Yard, Barry, followed by D604/3/2 on 29 July. *W. Potter/KRM*

BR Swindon/North British 2,000/2,200/2,400hp B-B

In what could be described as a classic picture advertising mid-1960s holiday rail travel in Devon, BR Swindon/North British B-B No D842 *Royal Oak* heads the 'Torbay Express' past Saltern Cove on 8 August 1962. Apart from bogie problems the D800s gave the WR excellent service with top speeds in excess of the authorised 90mph. It was brand new in December 1960, and just a shade over

eleven years after this picture was taken in October 1971, D842 was withdrawn along with the other remaining NBL built Class 43s, leaving only the last Swindon built Class 42s to linger on for little more than a year. Despite its relatively short life it went through the full green/maroon/blue repainting cycle at Swindon works.
W. Potter/KRM

TOP The down 'Torbay Express' passes through Starcross station behind BR Swindon/North British B-B No D819 *Goliath* on 29 August 1963. Public goods traffic was withdrawn from Starcross on 6 September 1965 and coal traffic ceased on 4 December 1967. The station became unstaffed on 3 May 1971 and the old station building was finally demolished in 1981. The footbridge, which had been erected in 1895, was replaced by the present structure in 1999. *W. Potter/KRM*

BOTTOM By 1964, the influx of both more powerful 'Western' diesel-hydraulics and Class 47s, drafted into the WR by BR's higher management, meant that some D800s were spared for use on the Waterloo–Exeter route. Here D820 *Grenville* is seen at Basingstoke in September 1965. *J. Davenport/MLS*

Before receiving any form of yellow warning panel, BR Swindon/North British B-B No D858 *Valorous* heads an up express through Bruton on Saturday 15 July 1961. The station is situated on the Bristol to Weymouth line some 32¾ miles south of Bath Spa. It opened in 1857, originally on the Wiltshire, Somerset and Weymouth line from Chippenham to Weymouth, as a single track line although Bruton was provided with a passing loop.

From 1906 an extension from Castle Cary to Taunton, coupled with improvements on the Berks and Hants extension railway (from Westbury to Reading) placed Bruton on the main Great Western line to the south west. The goods yard, seen behind the train, was on the north side of the line opposite the signal box, closed on 5 April 1965, and the station was downgraded to an unstaffed halt from 6 October 1969. *John Langford*

In 1963 control of the former SR lines in Devon and Cornwall was transferred from the Southern to the Western Region and rationalisation led to concentration of traffic on selected routes to avoid what was then seen as duplication. The GWR line from Paddington via Newbury and Somerton became the principal route to the West Country with the SR line from Waterloo reduced to secondary status. Here, BR Swindon B-B No D831 *Monarch* is captured with an up local west of Sidmouth Junction on 9 September 1964. The Western Region quickly replaced passenger Exeter to Waterloo steam traction in September 1964 with 'Warship' diesel hydraulic B-Bs, initially from Newton Abbot depot but later shared with Plymouth Laira. D829 *Magpie* was used for initial crew training duties at Salisbury shed, together with other examples later during the summer of 1964. In practice the Swindon built Maybach powered series (Class 42 D803-832, 866-870) were generally used but NBL built MAN engined Class 43 (D833-865) did appear infrequently in the earlier days. *David J. Mitchell*

North British Loco Co 1,000/1,100hp B-B

North British Loco Co B-B No D6335 is seen leaving Kingswear with an up working on 8 August 1962. At that time Dartmouth was being used for the start of The Tall Ships Race, the sail training ship *Amerigo Vespucci* being moored in the background. These locomotives were introduced as part of a plan to eliminate steam traction between Newton Abbot and Penzance, to be achieved with the introduction of approximately 130 diesel-hydraulic locomotives displacing an estimated 200 steam engines. After weighing and testing at Swindon, the first of

the class, D6300, entered traffic on 12 January 1959 when it took the 7.35am from Swindon to Bristol, continuing to work on local trips in the Bristol area for a further three weeks. Initially allocated to Plymouth Laira motive power depot for use in Devon and Cornwall, the D63XXs, on the main line, were invariably used in pairs. Contemporary reports suggested that there were insufficient trains capable of being worked by a single engine, but in practice the use of two locos in tandem was preferred.
W. Potter/KRM

The summer peace of the Forest of Dean is broken by the murmur of an 1100hp NBL/MAN engine as North-British B-B diesel-hydraulic No D6319 shunts Marsh Sidings at Parkend on 10 June 1968. The 3½ mile goods-only branch from Lydney Junction to Parkend came under threat of closure in 1970 and the Dean Forest Railway Society was formed with the ultimate aim of operating it as a steam tourist line. Initially the locomotives had some problems with engine and transmission faults, but could be returned to North British Locomotive Works for repair under the contractual agreement. By 1961, reliability had improved. By the mid 1960s, the locos had settled down to give reliable service, with availability over 85%. This class of loco, which eventually numbered some fifty-eight members, was more at home on secondary duties and local freight work, but with the closure of so many branch lines in the West Country, they became too numerous to retain in one area and were later to be seen all over WR territory, one of their final duties being the empty stock workings between Paddington and Old Oak Common. NBL went bankrupt in 1962 and, by the late 1960s, withdrawn locomotives were being used to provide spares. *W. Potter/KRM*

Beyer Peacock (Hymek) Ltd 1,700hp B-B

Hymek Type 3 B-B No D7070 trundles through Newport High Street station with a down freight on 2 February 1968. In the background the new GPO sorting office is under construction, a building that was later closed and sold into private ownership. Entering revenue earning service in the week commencing 10 July 1961, duties for this class were in the Bristol area. By October of that year sufficient experience had been gained with this class for D7023/4 to be entrusted with royal train duty when they were used to convey a royal party from Paddington to the new steel works at Llanwern where a short platform and canopy had been erected. Notable guests in the party were conveyed in two separate trains hauled by GWR King Class 4-6-0s No 6000 *King George V* and No 6018 *King Henry VI*, the latter carrying a 'R.T.B. Spencer Works' headboard. Operating on numerous cross-country routes, the 'Hymeks' fulfilled their role, handling many of the duties carried out by the GWR Castles, but their demise began with introduction of BR's Rationalisation Policy, many of the class being withdrawn in 1972, although a few survivors lingered on in traffic until 1975. *Bill Wright*

ABOVE After one year in traffic Hymek Type 3 B-B No D7037 is seen near Ledbury with a Hereford to Paddington train on 7 June 1963. Before the first locomotive was delivered the BTC was so confident with the design concept that they placed an order for a further 50 locomotives. Thus, in July 1960, ten months before delivery of the prototype, the order was increased to a total of 95 locomotives. One last batch of 6 was ordered in December 1961 – a total of 101 locomotives.

BELOW Another view of a Hymek Type 3 between Worcester and Hereford; this time D7076 is seen near Colwall with a Paddington to Hereford train on 1 June 1963. Many Hymeks remained in their original green livery until withdrawn. Becoming Class 35 under the TOPS renumbering scheme none of the class ever carried their five digit numbers although a few did lose their distinctive metal numerals. *Both: W. Potter/KRM*

Hymek Type 3 No D7030 has arrived at Strata Florida with the 12.00 train from Aberystwyth to Carmarthen on 14 June 1964. The station was about three miles from the old abbey of Strata Florida and Lord Lisburne of Trawsgoed, an influential local landowner, had tried to have the station named Ystrad Meurig after the village of that name.

The station was built at a point where it could serve three local villages, but its location made railway access difficult. The station itself was positioned on a tight curve, with the line from the south climbing inwards at 1 in 41, before exiting downwards on the branch line towards Aberystwyth at 1 in 43. The line between Aberystwyth and Carmarthen closed in two stages, the northern section closing prematurely in December 1964 when a section of the line one mile east of Llanilar was damaged by floods from the adjacent River Ystwyth. The remaining southern section closed to passengers in February 1965. Goods traffic continued in the form of milk trains from Carmarthen to Pont Llanio (just south of Tregaron) and the Felin Fach creamery (on the Aberaeron branch line) using Class 35 Hymek haulage until 1970 and with Class 37 haulage until the line closure in 1973.

David J. Mitchell

Hymek Type 3 No D7017 is seen in Sonning cutting with an express from Worcester on 11 May 1963. The first Hymek to arrive at Worcester for crew training duties was No D7076 of Cardiff Canton shed. The Hymek diesel locomotives took over about half of the Paddington express services during the summer 1963 timetable but were still working to steam locomotive schedules. With much ado British Railways heralded the end of steam working of passenger trains from Worcester to Paddington with a full press turn-out and sparkling 'Castle' Class 4-6-0 No.7023 *Penrice Castle* (of Worcester shed) on the 11.10 to London on 7 September, the last Saturday of operation of the Summer 1963 timetable. However, things did not go to plan. Major problems with the Western class diesel locomotives led to many steam substitutions as Hymek diesels had been moved to Cardiff.
Neville Simms

BR Swindon/Crewe 2,700hp C-C

BR Type 4 Diesel Hydraulic Western C-C No D1031 *Western Rifleman* is captured on film with Beyer Peacock (Hymek) Ltd B-B Type 3 No D7004 at Bristol Temple Meads on 30 August 1965. D1031 had received its maroon livery with small yellow ends on 20 December 1963, a colour scheme which it carried until 1 November 1968 when it was repainted in blue livery with full yellow ends. Initially replacing the Kings on the Paddington to Birmingham & Wolverhampton expresses, the Westerns suffered a high failure rate due in part to metal fatigue in the axles. When the London Midland took over the former GWR route north of Banbury there was an influx of Brush Type 4s, the Westerns being transferred to the South Wales line and to the West of England route. *Bill Wright*

BR Diesel Hydraulic Western C-C Type 4 No D1026 *Western Centurion* calls at Severn Tunnel Junction on 9 September 1965 with a South Wales to Paddington express. Released from Swindon works on 11 November 1966 after a bogie change – the works staff noted: 'RH loco nameplate missing – no action to be taken. Loco released with RH nameplate missing'. She ran in this condition until 30 May 1967 when she went into works for overhaul. She emerged on 14 June 1967 with a new nameplate fitted and painted into blue livery with full yellow ends. With the introduction of this class, passed for 90mph running, many of the WR's principal services were accelerated, one example being the South Wales Pullman which had its journey time reduced by fifteen minutes. One major change to this class commenced in 1968 when D1066 was fitted with air brakes. This was achieved by a reduction in the fuel tank at one end of the centre skirt, a large compressor being fitted transversely into this space. During their lifetime the Westerns slowly achieved a cult following, with many enthusiasts following their last workings in 1977. Such was their popularity that no fewer than seven examples survive in preservation. As with many other members of this class, D1026 was repainted in blue livery with full yellow ends, the only minor difference being that this loco did not carry the double arrow symbol on the 'A' end.
Bill Wright

1M95, the 11.50 Plymouth to Manchester express, prepares to run round its train at Newport High Street on 2 February 1968. It is being hauled by Diesel Hydraulic Western No D1017 *Western Warrior* which is carrying what has been described as a polychromatic blue livery. After the adoption of Rail Blue with full yellow ends in 1966 (D1048 was the first of the class painted in this livery), for some unexplained reason a small batch of locos (D1017, D1030, D1036, D1037, D1043, D1047 and D1057) received this variant married to small yellow warning panels; D1030 even carried red buffer beams for a short while. All other repaints were with full yellow ends which extended from the body line above the buffer beam up to the base of the window frames, along the sill of the cab-side windows onto the vertical end reveal. The valance above the cab windows on the front was also painted yellow, leaving the window frames in their base aluminium. The drive to repaint the locomotives in Rail Blue was outstripped by the safety directive dictating full yellow ends for all powered vehicles and some locomotives ran for a time with their original maroon bodies and full yellow ends. *Bill Wright*

Newly painted BR/Swindon 2,700 C-C Diesel Hydraulic No D1027 *Western Lancer* stands in Swindon works 'A' shop on 26 January 1964. D1001 was outshopped in a version of maroon livery while D1002 came out of shops in green livery with small yellow warning panels. Before too many more of the class were constructed a decision had to be made on the most attractive colour to be used. Rather than make the decision themselves the WR's Public Relations Department organised a competition in a well known railway periodical of the time and also among members of the staff. For the WR staff, details of the competition were announced through their monthly in-house magazine with the headline 'The chance of a footplate trip for spotters'. The prize for the winners of this competition would be for three railway enthusiasts, those whose names were first drawn out of the hat, to have a cab ride in a new Western Hydraulic. The winner, Gwen Bates of Newton Abbot, wrote with her entry "A trip in the driver's cab of an express has always been one of my most cherished ambitions". She also asked why was D1000's livery not called *Devon* Sand? *W. Potter/KRM*

BR/Crewe 2,700 C-C Diesel Hydraulic No D1056 *Western Sultan* heads a Gloucester to Paddington express near Ham Mill, Stroud, on 15 May 1965. D1056 is carrying the maroon livery with small yellow panels, a colour scheme it carried from 8 March 1963 until 15 September 1967 when it received full yellow ends. Initially the class was to be named after West Country beauty spots and the suggestion was that number D1000 was to become *Cheddar Gorge* before this proposal was dropped in favour of the *Western* names. By the late 1960s, apart from one or two engine problems, the Westerns were giving sterling service. The bogies were giving 150,000 miles between general repairs while the Voith transmission was shown to be a more reliable unit compared to the Mekydro transmission on the Warships. The class soldiered on into the early 1970s due to the unavailability of the English Electric Class 50 and, as maintenance staff had been told to keep the Westerns running without major repairs, it was not uncommon to see plumes of blue smoke from the locomotives' exhausts. Seven 'Westerns' have been saved for preservation, five of which were still in service until 28 February 1977. They are Nos D1010, D1013, D1015, D1023, D1041, D1048 and D1062. *W. Potter/KRM*

After just six months in traffic this detailed study shows BR/Swindon 2,700 C-C Diesel Hydraulic No D1004 *Western Crusader* in green livery as it awaits departure from Plymouth North Road on 10 August 1962. Together with D1002/3, D1004 was one of three members of this this class to initially carry the green livery before maroon was chosen by public vote as the standard colour for the class. This green livery was also chosen for Crewe built locos Nos D1035/6/7/8. Nos D1004/36/37 never carried maroon – going straight from green to BR Corporate Blue. The last locomotive to carry green was No D1038 *Western Sovereign* when it emerged from Crewe works on 7 September 1962. Working all the principal WR services in their heyday, and putting in some particularly good service on the Paddington to Birmingham route, the Westerns also performed some arduous tasks with freight. Eventually replaced by Class 47s on the Birmingham runs and Class 50s on West of England services, the class saw more frequent use on block oil trains and fully fitted stone trains although they could still handle passenger turns when required.
W. Potter/KRM

Birmingham Railway Carriage & Wagon Co 1,550hp Bo-Bo Type 3

A fascinating scene at Gravesend Central on Sunday 3 July 1960 as almost brand new BRCW Type 3 No D6511 appears on the 10.32am to Allhallows-on-Sea alongside the traditional 'H' Class 0-4-4Ts built some 55 years earlier. But the rolling stock continued to be vintage push-pull sets which were later supplemented by sets formed of Maunsell coaches. The locomotive crew must have welcomed the change from the usual primitive cab of a pre-Grouping steam loco to the comfort of a warm cab of a brand new diesel. In contrast the poor passengers had to put up with travelling in vintage push-pull sets. The BRCW Type 3s began service on the South Eastern Division of the Southern Region but rapidly spread across the whole Region and many were used much further afield – an example being the weekly Cliffe (Kent) to Uddingston (South Lanarkshire) cement train which was worked as far as York (and occasionally throughout) by pairs of these locomotives.
John Langford

ABOVE Another BRCW Type 3 on a Gravesend to Allhallows-on-Sea service. This time No D6514 is seen at Cliffe with the 2.38pm from Allhallows on Sunday 20 August 1961, the push-pull sets 616 and 619 made up from Maunsell coaches. At this time there appears to be active cement traffic from the nearby cement works. *John Langford*

BELOW In this picture taken on 2 July 1967, BRCW Type 3 No D6521 is seen leaving the 198yd Micheldever tunnel (also known as Litchfield tunnel) with a Waterloo to Weymouth service, the train including '4TC' units in BR blue livery. Preparations for third rail electrification are in progress, the track being energised to Bournemouth that year. *Neville Simms*

On the edge of the New Forest BRCW Bo-Bo Type 3 No D6512 is seen leaving Brockenhurst with the 10.45 Waterloo to Swanage in June 1965. Evidence of progress with electrification is visible with material for conductor rail being seen between the tracks. As a step towards the removal of steam from the Waterloo – Bournemouth services, D6580 was modified for remote operation with a modified rake of electric multiple unit stock and tested between Wimbledon Park & Basingstoke commencing on July 21 1965. The following month the newly delivered 4-TC stock was available for high speed testing on the Bournemouth line. The addition of the three jumpers on each side of the cab front of D6580 and the selection of a small rectangular yellow warning panel did not improve the aesthetics of the cab front. D6580 would later be modified to have its push-pull equipment conform to the other 18 locomotives similarly converted. These machines were always held in high regard, it being a great pity that the adherence to steam for train-heating purposes in the early 1960s precluded their wider use, and hence quantity production, for the other regions. A pleasing touch was the decision to name a few members of the class although an earlier scheme to name the whole class would appear to have been discarded.
P. Hutchinson/MLS

A truly evocative picture of Southern Region rail travel in the mid-1960s as BRCW Bo-Bo Type 3 No D6548 eases the 08.22 service from Waterloo to Bournemouth away from St Denys on 18 June 1966. Lineside observation on the South Western Division in the summer of 1966 found about one third of the locomotive hauled passenger services in the hands of Type 3s. The arrival of the winter season at the end of 1966 saw the Type 3s generally pulled from those passenger workings using steam heated stock. On the South Western Division, although there were more Brush Type 4s in use, the winter services still relied heavily on the dwindling steam fleet. As stock became available and various engineering works were completed further diagrams converted to Type 3s with 4TC stock, some being worked in push-pull mode. *J. Davenport/MLS*

English Electric Co 1,750hp Co-Co Type 3

It was unfortunate that the EE Type 3 Co-Co design was conceived when BR had adopted the four panel route indicator and before they had decided to abandon the use of gangway connections. This had given a somewhat untidy front end – features actually devised for EE's Type 4 1Co-Co1 D200 class diesels – the general appearance of the class being very similar to the the D200s. When new the livery was dark green without lining, the roof above the engine compartment mid grey, and black bogies and undergear. EE Type 3 No D6712 is seen on the GE at Cambridge on 31 May 1967 having been given a small yellow warning panel. *Bill Wright*

To provide adequate brake power on unfitted or partially fitted freight trains, BR produced the Diesel Brake Tenders, utilising old carriage bogies to carry a deadweight load encased in steel. Early versions had a rather square box shape, later versions being fitted with a streamlined casing. They were coupled to the locomotive but could be either pushed ahead of the loco or placed between the locomotive and the wagons. From the later 1960s the latter seems to have been the most common arrangement. Particularly heavy unfitted trains were sometimes supplied with two tenders, and these were usually positioned on either side of the locomotive. Brake tenders appeared in a range of liveries; green with red ends was one common scheme followed by all-over rail blue (mostly without any yellow on the ends) under the Corporate Livery. Brake tenders were phased out in the late 1970s as unfitted trains became increasingly rare. Here EE Type 3 No D6768 departs from Tees Yard with a train of loose-coupled 21-ton coal hoppers on 17 April 1967. The brake tender in front of the loco is utilising ex-LNER Gresley bogies.
Bill Wright

ABOVE EE Type 3 No D6715 is captured at Doncaster on 18 September 1965 with a train of empty carflats plus a Cartic-4 set for Dagenham. The Cartic-4 was a set of 4 wagons, semi-permanently coupled, with two decks that dipped between the bogies to provide adequate clearance within the loading gauge.

BELOW Brand new (only four days old) EE Type 3 No D6603 runs light engine through Burton on Trent en route to her new home at Landore on 20 September 1965. The last of the class, No D6608, was delivered in November 1965. *Both: Bill Wright*

Released from English Electric Vulcan Foundry with Works Number EE/VF3385/D851 and first allocated to Landore in November 1963, D6907 is captured with a freight in Ebbw Vale near Crumlin Low Level on 3 August 1967. The line closed to passenger traffic on 30 April 1962, prior to the Beeching Axe, with the mineral branches following on 7 April 1969 and the Talywain branch on 3 May 1980. Freight services to and from the steelworks at Ebbw Vale continued until the site closed on 5 July 2002. The final freight service to run from the Corus steelworks in Ebbw Vale in 2003 removed scrap metal from site. Passenger train services were restored to the line after a gap of 46 years on 6 February 2008, between a new station at Ebbw Vale Parkway and Cardiff Central, the first train of the restored service leaving Cardiff Central for Ebbw Vale Parkway at 06:35.
W. Potter/KRM

In this somewhat sad but still fascinating picture taken at Wakefield Kirkgate on 17 May 1968, EE Type 3 No D6739 is hauling condemned steam locomotives on their final journey for breaking at Draper's yard in Hull. In the consist are three Stanier 8F 2-8-0s, Nos 48307, 48700 and 48740 in addition to Stanier Class 5 4-6-0 No 45294. On the left of the picture at the far end of the station is another EE Type 3, No D6945. No D6739 rolled off the Vulcan Foundry's production line at Newton-le-Willows in May 1962 and was allocated to Hull Dairycoates (53A) mpd. What was probably its first revenue earning duty came on 9 June 1962 when it worked the 17.17 Hull to Kings Cross as far as Doncaster. With British Railways' avidness to eliminate steam traction as soon as possible, several repeat orders for EE Type 3s were placed with the Vulcan Foundry until a total of 309 of the type had been ordered. The Vulcan Foundry was working at full capacity to complete this large order, much of the work was being subcontracted to Robert Stephenson & Hawthorns at Darlington, where factory space was available. The first locomotive to be completed was No D6700, and on 2 December 1960 it was officially allocated to Stratford (30A) mpd. The last of the class, No D6608, was delivered in November 1965. Becoming No 37308 under TOPS, then carrying No 37274 from 1989–2000, No 37308 survives in preservation.
Bill Wright

Split headcode EE Type 3 No D6817 has received full yellow ends in this picture taken at Manchester Piccadilly on 14 June 1968 as it prepares to depart with the boat train for Harwich. In early BR days the Harwich boat train connected Liverpool Central with Harwich via Manchester Central (reverse) with a change of locomotive there and another at Guide Bridge after traversing the 'Fallowfield Loop'. Electric traction over Woodhead to Sheffield followed and then diesel haulage throughout via Lincoln and March (GN&GE Joint). After closure of Manchester Central (1969), trains were diverted to Manchester Piccadilly where they terminated, English Electric Type 3s being rostered to run throughout. By the 1980s new Sprinter DMUs brought much more frequent services from North West England into East Anglia making a special train to Harwich redundant (along with the complexities of privatisation). Having said that there was one final attempt to emulate the past when a connection from Glasgow re-appeared from 16 May 1983 with the title of *The European* and operated with portions from Glasgow and Edinburgh being married up at Carstairs, leaving Manchester for Harwich at 15.02. *Bill Wright*

English Electric Co 3,300hp Co-Co 'Deltic' Type 5

Having entered traffic on 22 June 1961, EE Type 5 'Deltic' No D9007 *Pinza* is seen at Grantham with a passenger train from Hull to Kings Cross on 7 January 1962. Some three weeks earlier, on 4 June, D9007 had been fitted with experimental warning horns inserted into the nose cones of both No 1 and No 2 ends. On 5 January 1969 D9007 had the dubious honour of hauling 1Z28, an RCTS organised Leeds – Edinburgh railtour via the Waverley route, being the last day of operation over the line and 1Z28, the Edinburgh – Leeds return. Many of the passengers on the train were unaware of the protests that would take place, D9007 being slowed to a walking pace on the climb towards Whitrope summit from Riccarton Junction – the rails had been greased. Members of an unknown border faction could be seen dancing on a distant hillside. Elsewhere, protesters donned top-hats, and, complete with a black coffin, proclaimed the economic decline that would result from closure. The coffin, addressed to Richard Marsh, then Transport Minister, was put on the last southbound train. *Neville Simms*

EE Type 5 'Deltic' No D9004 *Queen's Own Highlander* takes the Bradford portion of the 16.10 'White Rose Pullman' away from Bradford Exchange on 29 May 1966. The 'White Rose Pullman' ran from Kings Cross to Leeds and Bradford between 1964 and 1967 utilising the stock from The 'Queen of Scots'. D9004 was named *Queen's Own Highlander* in a ceremony at Inverness on 23 May 1964 and returned south with the 17.45 Inverness to Euston, 'The Royal Highlander', as far as Perth. Some three months after this picture was taken in July 1966 D9004 was recorded on a breakdown train, 1Z99 Gateshead Shed to Alnmouth Yard. No exact date was recorded; however, it was reported as the only spare loco on Gateshead (52A) mpd and took the breakdown crane to Alnmouth due to a derailment in the coal road. Some years later D9004 was to return to Inverness for the two-day Inverness TMD open days on 9/10 June 1973. Once again it returned south on 10 June with the 19.00 Inverness – Euston, 'The Royal Highlander' to Perth piloting a Class 24 and a Class 26 locomotive. *David J. Mitchell*

This classic scene at Wakefield Westgate on
6 June 1967 depicts EE Type 5 No D9009 *Alycidon*
as it works the 11.55 from Bradford to Kings Cross.
The Deltic locomotives based at Edinburgh and
Newcastle were named after local army regiments
but the eight Deltics allocated to the Eastern region,
and maintained at Finsbury Park depot, took the
names of race horses, including five Derby winners.
D9009 was named at Doncaster works without
ceremony on 21 July 1961 *Alycidon* in honour of
the racehorse owned by the 17th Earl of Derby,
winning the Ascot Cup, Goodwood Cup, Corporation
Stakes and Doncaster Cup, and whose offspring
included Meld who won the Oaks, the 1000 Guineas
and the St Leger (the triple crown for fillies).
Other locos named after Derby winners were
Nimbus (1949), *Tulyar* (1952) *Pinza* (1953),
Crepello (1957) and *St Paddy* (1960). Completing
the stud were *Meld, Ballymoss* and *Alycidon*.
Following withdrawal on 2 January 1982 this loco
was preserved by the Deltic Preservation Society
(DPS) and has been mostly based at the DPS depot at
Barrow Hill. It was recertified for mainline use in
July 2012. *Bill Wright*

ABOVE Having entered traffic in March 1962, EE Type 5 No D9021 *Argyll & Sutherland Highlander* is seen at Wakefield with 1E10, the 11.40am Harrogate to Kings Cross, in March 1966. The last of the production series of Deltic diesels, No D9021 was considered to be the test loco of the fleet and its on loan transfer from Haymarket to Finsbury Park from 12th November until 19th June 1965 coincided with the ER carrying out certain tests for the fleet. D9021 was cut-up at Doncaster works in September 1982, the No 1 end cab being privately preserved. *Derek Huntriss*

BELOW With a down train having just cleared the platform the photographer has captured EE Type 5 Deltic No D9019 *Royal Highland Fusilier* carrying the 'Winged Thistle' headboard as it brings 1A35, the 10.00 Edinburgh to Kings Cross 'Flying Scotsman', through Doncaster station on 18 September 1966. Exactly one week earlier at a ceremony at Glasgow Central, D9019 was the last member of the class to receive a name. A crest from this loco sold at Great Central Railwayana Auctions on 13 July 2013 for £4500. *Bill Wright*

Clayton Equipment Co 900hp Bo-Bo Type 1

Centre cab 'Claytons' Nos D8526 and D8529 are depicted approaching Beattock prior to shunting an up goods working into the yard on 5 October 1963. Delivery of the 900hp D8500 took place at Marylebone on 26 July 1962, the locomotive returning to Derby the next day. Intended for use on the Scottish Region, D8500 arrived at Polmadie on 10 September 1962; the class was to replace the veteran 'Jumbos' on their various trip workings. On 5 September 1963, D8500/1 worked in tandem on a trial iron-ore train from Tyne Dock to Consett, further trials being conducted later in the month on coal trains over the Blyth and Tyne section. On 4 December that year, newly delivered D8555 was a runaway casualty whilst working trip E58 on the Loanhead branch, becoming derailed and causing a line blockage. The Claytons, as they became known, were never a success. Major problems with the Paxman engines resulted in availability being as low as 50%, their problems reaching such a pitch that newly constructed locos were being placed directly into store. Coupled with this, the work for which they were designed, namely light to medium freight, was disappearing as a result of the Beeching Plan. When the BRB's National Traction Plan was implemented the Claytons were early victims, all being withdrawn by the end of 1971. *David J. Mitchell*

Clayton Type 1 No D8613 is pictured at Glapwell Colliery in north-east Derbyshire assisting Midland 4F 0-6-0 No 43953. No D8613 had been attached at Foxlow Junction to assist No 43953 up to the colliery. Here the pair have run round the train ready to return to Foxlow Junction. This tour commemorated the virtual end of the once numerous fleet of Midland 0-6-0 tender locomotives. The six coach train visited numerous lines in the heart of the Midland system, where the 0-6-0s were once so common. Such was the rarity at that time of the 4Fs that No 43953 had to be brought in from Workington shed to power the train. This machine would in fact prove to be the last Midland 4F in service, retirement coming about three weeks later on 6 November. Whilst prepared to the highest standard for the rail tour it became obvious towards the end that all was not well with 43953, with time being lost and the speed rarely exceeding 30mph. Perhaps the 50mph streak on the Ambergate to Derby section overstretched the forty-four year old veteran.

The 4F is paired with an LMS tender, possibly from a scrapped LMS compound. The author's uncle was one of the fitting team who had prepared the 4F at Workington mpd and was most disappointed when it didn't return. *Neville Simms*

Brush/Sulzer 2,750hp (now 2,580hp), 2,650hp Co-Co Type 4

ABOVE Passing the site of the closed Portsmouth station on the climb from leaving the Calder Valley line at Stansfield Hall Junction to Copy Pit summit, Brush/Sulzer Type 4 No D1881 is heading a Wakes Weeks excursion to Blackpool in 1965. Few traces of the station remain today, although the line itself remains in use for passenger trains between York and Blackpool via Leeds. *David J. Mitchell*

RIGHT It is hard to believe that today's ECML once looked like this as Brush Type 4 No D1526 is seen at Peterborough with an up coal train on 7 October 1968. Wagons three and four in the consist are post-1966 rebuilds of unfitted 16-ton mineral wagons to Diagram 1/108. No D1526 was built at Brush, Loughborough, entered traffic on 21 June 1963 and allocated to Finsbury Park MPD. It survived in traffic for twenty eight years until withdrawn in May 1991. *Bill Wright*

ABOVE Brush Type 4 No D1851 (TOPS No 47201) is on the up fast line at Carnforth on 30 March 1967 with a Freightliner working. The 'Liner Train' service proposed by Dr Beeching to operate scheduled inter-city services transporting ISO standard containers was authorised in 1964. The name Freightliners was in use, and painted on the containers, by 1965 and in 1968 Freightliners Ltd was established as a separate company from British Railways operating as part of the National Freight Corporation (NFC) which was essentially the less-than-wagon load railway business spun off as a separate entity in 1969. *Peter Fitton*

BELOW Brush Type 4 No 1896 (TOPS No 47377) waits near Blackwell to descend the Lickey incline with a train of sheeted wagons in July 1970. The normal procedure when loose coupled steam hauled freights used to descend the 1 in 37 to Bromsgrove was that the guard and brakesman conferred. Then the signal to proceed was given and the train moved slowly forward whilst wagon brakes were applied. After this the fireman would look back to see that the guard had rejoined his brake van, whereupon hand signals were exchanged. If appropriate the fireman would apply the tender handbrake and the driver the engine brake. *J. Tarrant/KRM*

When Merry-Go-Round (MGR) services were first introduced, British Rail designed an all-new wagon with air brakes and a capacity for 33 tonnes of pulverised coal. The prototype was a 32 ton unit and was built at Darlington and tested in 1964. Before the introduction of TOPS these wagons were referred to by the telegraphic code name 'HOP AB 33' which was an abbreviation of Hopper Air Brake 33 tonne. With the introduction of TOPS in 1973 the wagons were given the code 'HAA'. Here Brush Type 4

No D1882 heads south through Doncaster station with a train of clean MGRs on 8 February 1968. Locomotives used on the MGR trains needed to be fitted with electronic speed control known as Slow Speed Control, so that the driver could engage the system and the train could proceed at a fixed very slow speed under the loading and unloading facilities. The system was originally fitted to some members of Class 20, Class 26 and Class 47. *Bill Wright*

English-Electric Co 2,700hp Co-Co Type 4

By March 1964, Crewe works had ceased to give general overhauls to steam locomotives, the largest being a heavy intermediate. Concurrently most locomotive depots were running down their steam locomotives and the condition of many deteriorated due to inferior maintenance. Depots such as Carlisle Kingmoor often had as many as thirty engines stopped for repair. As a stop gap, before full electrification on the LM main line between Weaver Junction and Glasgow, fifty English Electric locomotives were ordered. These 2,700hp machines, based on the privately sponsored prototype DP2, were the final example of high speed mixed traffic diesel electric locomotives to be built for BR. On a miserable 12 March 1968 EE Type 4 No D405 calls at Warrington Bank Quay with the 08.20 Birmingham New Street to Perth 'Midland Scot'. The train had left Birmingham behind BR/EE Class AL6 No E3145 (later Class 86/0 No 86014) which was replaced at Crewe by No D405. *Bill Wright*

EE Type 4 No D400 has returned from a test working over the Settle & Carlisle line from Carlisle and is seen at Farington Junction near Preston on 20 September 1967. On the skyline can be seen the coaling tower at Lostock Hall (10D) mpd. By 1 October 1967 this locomotive had arrived at Crewe for acceptance trials. In addition to the usual works plates, D400 carried a small oval plate inscribed 'This locomotive is the property of English Electric Holdings', who leased them to BR. During February 1968, D402 had arrived at Polmadie for crew training. The multiple control jumpers had not been fitted on locomotives D402-D449 although wiring was installed for subsequent fitting. Having been introduced into regular traffic, sister engine D401 was working the down 'Royal Scot' on 25 April 1968 when it came to grief only a mile short of its goal and was derailed at a pair of facing points at the north end of Eglinton Street station. With local services more or less at a standstill, the Polmadie and Eastfield cranes had No D401 rerailed by 21.00. Locomotive crews found the D400s had good high speed performance and were able to maintain speeds of 100mph, but initially their availabilty in traffic was poor with engine problems. These problems required new cylinder heads to be fitted both at Crewe works and the Vulcan Foundry. Prior to the completion of electrification work on the West Coast Main Line the class were able to give a good account of themselves. *Peter Fitton*

Blue Pullmans

Taken at Paddington on 16 April 1964 this picture shows Blue Pullmans side by side. On the left is the unit being prepared to depart for Birmingham and on the right is the South Wales Pullman. There were two versions, built by Metro Cammell in Birmingham: two first-class six-car sets for the London Midland Region (LMR), and three two-class eight-car sets for the Western Region (WR). They were initially operated by the luxury train operator, The Pullman Car Company, which the British Transport Commission (BTC) had recently acquired. In 1962, three years after their introduction, Pullman was nationalised, and operation was incorporated into the British Railways network.

Originally given the last Pullman vehicle numbers the trains gained the British Rail TOPS classification of Class 251 (motor cars) and Class 261 (kitchen and parlour cars), although they never carried these numbers. With a power car at each end the coach bodies measured 66ft 6ins x 9ft 3ins anticipating introduction of the High Speed Train. The NB/MAN engines were initially unreliable although this didn't affect their popularity with the travelling public, giving a mediocre but very quiet ride. The sets were only made redundant by the introduction of the Mk II loco hauled carriage and the Euston to Birmingham electrification.
David J. Mitchell

Bringing luxurious and air-conditioned standards of comfort to the British rail traveller, seats on the Blue Pullmans commanded supplementary fares. There were two different decorative schemes in the first class saloons: one had grey walls, blue and navy striped upholstery, a red/black carpet and polished ebony partitions, while the other had grey walls, red and navy striped upholstery, a blue and black carpet and polished rosewood partitions. Here the 11.15 St Pancras to Nottingham Midland Pullman passes through Trent on 17 September 1965. This train, consisting only of first-class Pullman cars, afforded cushioned comfort for passengers taking a leisurely luncheon as the train cruised north to Nottingham. With two stops along the way, the Midland Pullman reached Nottingham in just two hours. Beeching's cuts and the demotion of the Midland Main Line to secondary status meant that St Pancras lost some of its importance. *Bill Wright*

First Generation DMUs

The first eight sets of 'Derby Lightweight' two-car DMUs were built for an intensive local service introduced between Leeds and Bradford. Here a two-car Derby Lightweight set is seen at Ribblehead station as it prepares to depart as the 11.55am all stations service from Hellifield to Carlisle. Additional units were introduced in West Cumberland providing services from Carlisle to Silloth, Whitehaven, Workington and Penrith. To obtain a satisfactory power to weight ratio with these units it was decided to construct the railcars integrally of light alloy. Eight two-car sets were made at Derby for the West Riding scheme and a further thirteen for services in West Cumberland. Each two-car set seated 114 second-class and sixteen first-class passengers. Later builds had seating variations. *Peter Fitton*

ABOVE Comprising 1, 2 and 4-car units the Derby Lightweights were intended to replace push-pull steam trains on the LMR. Whilst a single unit would be sufficient to meet weekday demand on Banbury (Merton St) to Buckingham services, on Saturdays two units could be required. Here M79900 and M79901 are seen at Banbury (Merton Street) on 4 July 1959. Today M79900 survives in preservation on the Ecclesbourne Valley Railway. *John Langford*

BELOW It is most unlikely that many of the passengers on the leading units of this train would believe they were travelling by Rolls-Royce. The 'Calder Valley' DMUs (later Class 110) were powered by four 180hp Rolls-Royce engines which ranked them amongst the most interesting DMUs on British Rail. With the south stand of Blackpool football club behind the train, this Class 110 unit is passing Bloomfield signal box on 25 September 1962. *Peter Fitton*

This 2-car Class 120 DMU is seen entering Church Stretton with a service for Hereford on 7 June 1965. British Railways placed the order with British United Traction in summer 1956 for the equipment required for the 98 power cars and 47 trailers of the first batch. The order, along with equipment ordered by Cravens for 66 power cars and the 3 parcels cars, was valued at £830,000. The first batch was ordered for the WR's West Country dieselisation scheme, which it hoped to complete by the end of 1959. The sets were expected to work between Bristol and South Devon. Their general reliability and good braking characteristics made them popular with drivers. Some of the WR sets had a powerful headlight fitted between the two cab front windows, for use when operating over the Central Wales line. Economies made by Dr Richard Beeching put paid to numerous cross-country lines, resulting in a number of these units being switched from one area to another, the cuts also spelling the end for the small buffet car portion of the trailer which was considered too costly to operate. Some of the London Midland Region's units were transferred to Scotland in the mid-1980s, mainly finding use on local services from Edinburgh (notably to North Berwick). The final vehicles survived until 1989. Trailer Second No M59276 is preserved at the Great Central Railway. *J.D. Darby/MLS*

The interior of Seaton station on 10 June 1964 with an unidentified Class 122 single-unit railcar having travelled the 4½-mile branch line from Seaton Junction. For operation with these single unit railcars the Gloucester Railway Carriage & Wagon Co built nine driving trailer seconds (with cab at one end only) for use when passenger loads exceeded the capacity of a single car. The platforms here had been extended by the Southern Railway in 1937 to cope with the additional summer traffic. With intermediate stopping stations at Colyton and Colyford the line sprang into life when holidaymakers descended from London – even until 1963 there were through coaches on three separate trains from Waterloo. Listed for closure in the Beeching Report, the introduction of dmus to work the line was to no avail; the line had already lost its goods traffic when final closure came on 7 March 1966. No fewer than eight of the Class 122 units survive in preservation. Today, the 2ft 9in gauge Seaton Tramway carries holidaymakers in miniature electric trams from its terminus at Seaton along the trackbed of the line beside the peaceful estuary of the River Axe to Colyton. *J.D. Darby/MLS*

ABOVE In this 3 September 1964 picture taken at Seaton Junction the branch service to Seaton has been strengthened to two Class 122 single unit railcars, W56298W leading. Today the station (now a private house), down platform and footbridge survive. *David J. Mitchell*

BELOW GWR railcar No W26W forms the 12.10pm Woofferton to Kidderminster service on 18 March 1961 and is seen at the long-forgotten railway junction at Cleobury Mortimer where passengers once left on the Cleobury Mortimer and Ditton Priors Light Railway. *John Langford*

ABOVE This Gloucester Railway Carriage & Wagon Co Class 100 DMU forms the 4pm service to Birmingham New Street as it waits to depart from Stockport on 11 September 1965. There were 40 power cars and 40 trailers in this class, all in twin unit formations, the original allocations being to both the London Midland and Scottish regions. Unfortunately this class has not fared well in preservation. Seven cars entered preservation of which only four now exist. *Wallace Sutherland/MLS*

BELOW This afternoon Manchester Piccadilly to Macclesfield service formed of a two car Metropolitan-Cammell unit was photographed at Longsight in June 1957. The station closed on 15 September 1958, very little of it remaining today. A short platform has been built on part of the former station site for the use of railway staff travelling to and from the adjacent carriage depot. *Colour-Rail*

Shortly before closure to passengers of the four miles seventy-five chains branch from Keighley on 30 December 1961 this Derby-built twin unit (later Class 108) has arrived at Oxenhope station. The British Rail Class 108 diesel multiple units were built by BR Derby from 1958 to 1961, with a final production quantity of 333 vehicles. These units stayed in regular service until 1990, when they began to be withdrawn from traffic. The final units lasted in traffic until October 1993, although many saw further use in departmental service, as Sandite or route-learner units. After British Railways closed this line in 1962, local people and railway enthusiasts joined forces to save it. A preservation society was formed and after many years of volunteer struggle the line re-opened to passenger traffic on 29 June 1968. In the years since reopening not only has the Keighley & Worth Valley Railway developed into one of the country's premier 'heritage' railways it has continued a tradition of service to the communities along the Worth Valley, operating rail services on almost 200 days per year. *David J. Mitchell*

Bristol Commercial Vehicles provided the chassis for two railbuses (SC 79958/9) in 1958. Each used a Gardner 112 horsepower (84 kW) engine and a hydraulic automatic transmission. The bodywork was built by Eastern Coach Works. They were used on branch lines in Scotland, but no further orders were placed and the pair were withdrawn and scrapped in 1968. SC79958 was officially introduced on the 51 mile Speyside route between Elgin, Granton-on-Spey and Aviemore, on 3 November 1958, working a daily diagram of around 300 miles. As with steam there were three services each way, and an extra train on a Saturday. One return journey was extended to Keith Junction and one to Elgin. Here unit No SC 79959 is seen awaiting departure from Crieff with the service to Gleneagles on 22 July 1963. *David J. Mitchell*

A Class 108 Derby-built twin unit leads this formation on a Morecambe to Leeds service as it passes Settle Junction on 12 March 1966. Prior to January 1966 the Leeds to Morecambe service used the 'Little' North Western Railway route via Lancaster, with the Furness & Midland Joint line to Carnforth served mainly by through carriages detached from/attached to main line trains at Wennington (although a small number of local trains operated between there and Carnforth only). The Beeching Report of 1963 deemed this service pattern unsatisfactory and proposed that services be 'modified', with the original route from Wennington to Lancaster and Morecambe eventually being closed in favour of the F&MJ line on 3 January 1966. From that date all trains ran via Carnforth, the WCML, Hest Bank North Junction and the former LNWR Morecambe Branch Line to reach their destination. This routeing had one major drawback in that travellers could no longer reach Lancaster directly, instead having to change at Carnforth onto Furness Line services – a situation that would remain unchanged until the early 1980s. Freight services on the route ended in 1986 following the closure of the Heysham chemical plant, leaving the Leeds to Lancaster/Morecambe passenger service as the only regular user – a situation that remains unchanged to the present day. *David J. Mitchell*

A Birmingham Railway Carriage & Wagon Co 3-car Class 110 unit is seen passing Gelderd Junction in Leeds with a service from Harrogate to Leeds Central on 18 February 1967. Behind the leading car can be seen the Grade II listed roundhouse built for the Leeds and Thirsk Railway Company which later amalgamated with the Leeds and Selby and the York and North Midland to become the North Eastern Railway. The roundhouse was designed with a single entrance track with 20 stabling bays radiating around a central turntable measuring approximately 12.75 metres (42ft 6ins) in diameter. By 1889 the roundhouse was too small for larger modern engines and was closed. It was then used as a drill hall for the Leeds Rifles until 1916 before becoming the home of Marshalls Engineers. Leeds Commercial Ltd van and truck hire, who have occupied the property since 1969, invite the public to view the roundhouse during National Heritage Weekend each year and the historical information provided here is taken from a leaflet supplied at one of these events. *David J. Mitchell*

Diesel Shunters

This view taken at Perth on 16 July 1965 sees three Andrew Barclay 204hp 0-4-0 diesel shunting locos Nos D2412, D2444 and D2411 alongside LMS Stanier Class 5 4-6-0s No 44698 and 44779 whilst English Electric 2,000hp 1Co-Co1 No D265 passes with a Euston to Perth express. The Scottish Region had identified a need for a powerful short wheelbase locomotive which would be able to be used for short trip workings as well as shunting wagons. An 0-4-0 with a 7ft wheelbase and powered by the same engine that was used in the 0-6-0 classes was designed by

Andrew Barclay 35 locomotives of the type seen here were delivered between 1958 and 1960. Fitted with vacuum braking for train working these powerful 0-4-0s proved their worth in Scotland. Whilst withdrawals commenced in 1967 some of the class carried TOPS numbers and survived in traffic until 1981. A single locomotive survives, number 06003. It was the last locomotive of the class in service, and was transferred to the departmental fleet, renumbered 97804, and used at the Reading Signal Works. *Bill Wright*

Taken one day before the previous picture, North British Loco Co 0-4-0 diesel hydraulic shunting loco No D2771 is captured at Parkhead (65C) mpd in Glasgow. In the shadows to the left of this loco, not clearly visible, is the former Highland Railway 'Jones Goods' 4-6-0 No 103. As seen in this example, on locos from No D2754 onwards the bodywork was altered to have a stepped-height bonnet in front of the cab windows. A rubber seal separated this from the front, lower, bonnet portion. More visible in this picture is the wire mesh guard in front of the cab footsteps, protecting the drive crank. Most of this class were withdrawn in 1967/8 but two survive in preservation, No D2767 at the Bo'ness and Kinneil Railway and No D2774 at the Strathspey Railway. *Bill Wright*

Until the early 1960s, shunting duties in the docks at Southampton had been the preserve of fourteen 'USA' class 0-6-0 steam locomotives. In the early 1960s a similar number of diesel electric engines were ordered from Ruston & Hornsby specifically for use in the Southern Region's Southampton docks complex. These were to replace the war surplus 0-6-0s that had been puchased in 1946. Here No D2987 is seen at work in August 1965. These neat looking engines were initially supplied in the Southern Region's malachite green livery with red and white lining, grey cab roof, black wheels and undergear. This class was notorious for having the axleboxes running hot when travelling at high speed.

This characteristic was initially encountered during delivery of the first locomotive, and subsequent deliveries were made by road. A later trial move of one Class 07 to Selhurst depot for tyre profiling also resulted in overheating axlebox problems and all subsequent moves of any distance, particularly those to BREL workshops, were made by road. This is in contrast to other shunter classes that would commonly have had their side-rods removed and traction motors isolated and would then form part of a train heading in the appropriate direction. Class 08s were commonly moved in this fashion at up to 35 mph (56 km/h) – overnight wagon-load trains being utilised if possible. *F. Hornby*

Another Class 07 0-6-0 diesel shunter, No D2989, is seen near the dock entrance in Canute Road on 15 September 1966, the train being preceded by a man with a red flag who was in place to stop traffic at the cross roads. The members of the class that had TOPS numbering applied were also equipped with high-level air brake pipes, allowing them to move Southern Region Electric Multiple Units, and three locomotives were used at Bournemouth EMU depot for a period. This was not their principal work but they were often employed around their home-depot on general shunting duties. They were relatively fast for shunters and it was envisaged that they would be used to trip local traffic to/from Southampton docks. Accordingly they were equipped, from new, with mainline headcode marker lights (six for the SR). D2989 was sold to ICI Wilton, Middlesbrough in 1976 and is now preserved at the Great Central Railway at Loughborough.
Neville Simms

The British Rail Class 14 is a type of small diesel-hydraulic locomotive built in the mid-1960s. Twenty-six of these 0-6-0 locomotives were ordered in January 1963, and were built at British Railways Swindon works. The anticipated work for this class was yard shunting, trip work (between local yards) and short-distance freight trains. The order was expanded to 56 in mid-1963, before work had started on the first order. The Class 14s, like many other early types of diesel, had an extremely short life with British Railways, in this case not because of poor reliability but because many of its envisaged duties disappeared on the BR network a few years after they came into use. Most were resold for industrial use, where the vast majority had a working life of two to three times that with British Railways. Here No D9555, the last to be constructed, is seen with a brake van tour in the Forest of Dean at Whitecliffe Quarry on 26 April 1967. Today this locomotive is privately owned and operates on the Dean Forest Railway, Gloucestershire, its original route. *W. Potter/KRM*

BR Class 14 diesel hydraulic 0-6-0 No D9526 heads a train of empty coal wagons through Gloucester Eastgate station in 1967. After 1968, the station was rationalised. The island platform was lengthened at the Barton Street end and the tracks were removed from the other two platforms. The extensive goods yard and sidings were also lifted at this time. Colour light track circuit block signalling was installed and the station was effectively merged with Gloucester Central. Eastgate station closed on 1 December 1975, along with the Tuffley Loop. This was partly an attempt by British Rail to cut maintenance costs and partly a result of pressure from the road lobby and local councillors who wanted to rid Gloucester of four of its level crossings. Services that had previously called at Eastgate now had to perform a reversal at Central station, an operational inconvenience that has led to fewer trains calling at Gloucester. As the rebuilt Gloucester Central station was not completed until 1977, the administrative offices on Eastgate station lingered on in use for nearly two more years until demolition came in 1977. The site is now an Asda supermarket. Only a very few traces of the former Tuffley Loop can now be found.
W. Potter/KRM

ABOVE The Class 03 shunter shares, with the Class 04, the reputation of one of BR's most successful smaller 0-6-0 diesel-mechanical shunters. The class of 230 examples was built by British Railways' Swindon and Doncaster works in 1957-1962 and numbered D2000-D2199 and D2370-D2399. Nos D2009-D2012 are seen at Swindon in February 1958.
T .B. Owen/Colour-Rail

BELOW Class 03 No D2141 is seen at Hemyock with milk tankers on 2 September 1964. There were two sidings into the dairy, both crossing the road. With locomotives not being allowed to cross the road, the dairy staff winched the tanks into the milk factory and ran them back to the station by gravity.
David J. Mitchell

Taken at Craiginches North (Aberdeen) on 17 June 1965 this picture shows BR/English Electric Class 08 shunter No D3548 on a trip working to the yard adjacent to the station. As the standard general-purpose diesel shunter on BR, almost any duty requiring shunting would involve a Class 08. The class became a familiar sight at many major stations and freight yards. However, since their introduction, the nature of rail traffic in Britain has changed considerably.

Freight trains are now mostly fixed rakes of wagons and passenger trains are mostly multiple units, neither requiring the attention of a shunting locomotive. Consequently, a large proportion of the class has been withdrawn from mainline use and stored, scrapped, exported or sold to industrial or heritage railways. The locomotives were built at the BR works of Crewe, Darlington, Derby, Doncaster and Horwich between 1952 and 1962. *Derrick Codling*

Less than one year old, Drewry Car Co 204hp 0-6-0 diesel-mechanical shunter (later TOPS Class 04) No 11224 is depicted outside Hither Green (73C) mpd on 8 March 1958. However, the first locomotive to be built to this design was actually DS1173 in 1948, which served as a departmental shunter at Hither Green depot. The Class 04 locomotives were supplied by the Drewry Car Co, which at the time had no manufacturing capability. Drewry sub-contracted the construction work to two builders, both of whom built other locomotives under the same arrangement. Early locomotives (including DS1173) were built by Vulcan Foundry and later examples were built by Robert Stephenson and Hawthorns. *W. Potter/KRM*

Seen outside Swindon (82C) mpd on 9 September 1961 is former GWR diesel electric 0-6-0 shunter No 15100. The GWR had decided to evaluate the merits of the 0-6-0 diesel-electric shunting locomotive for themselves, ordering this solitary prototype from Hawthorn Leslie in 1935. It was a 0-6-0 diesel electric shunter, with a close family resemblance to the Southern Railway Maunsell 350 hp diesel mechanical shunter. It was renumbered 15100 by British Rail in 1948, finally working at Bristol and Swindon before withdrawal in 1965. At one stage in its career it carried experimental black and white striped warning ends and is seen here having received the standard black and yellow version with a full set of electric marker lights being affixed to each end. With the exception of two GWR locomotives which were in fully lined green, the pre-war diesel shunters were in black, and during the war period the War Department allocation were in drab shades of khaki or green. After the war black was again favoured, except by the GWR who used plain green devoid of pre-war orange and black lining-out. *Neville Simms*

One of 120 members of this class, Hunslet Engine Co 204hp 0-6-0 diesel mechanical shunter No D2581 is depicted in the shed yard at Thornton Junction (62A) mpd on 16 July 1965. Using a more modern design than some diesel shunters, although some would say it went a little too far with its vast window areas of complex shapes, it had remarkably narrow doors, a feature which must have caused some moments of distress for more rotund BR drivers. These were successful machines with a solitary example remaining in departmental service on the Isle of Wight until 1983. As for other members of this class the National Traction Plan saw them as surplus to BR needs and they were withdrawn between 1966 and 1968. Two others, Nos D2612 and D2615 (departmental Nos 88/89) continued for some years. Five locomotives of this type have been preserved: D2554 *Nuclear Fred* at the Isle of Wight Steam Railway, D2578 *Cider Queen*, privately preserved by the D2578 Locomotive Group at Moreton Business Park, Herefordshire, D2587 by Heritage Shunters Trust and D2595 at the Ribble Steam Railway.
Bill Wright

This picture, taken at Halifax North Bridge Goods Yard on 28 May 1963, sees Class 08 No D3151 at work in the Gas Works sidings with ex-WD 2-8-0 No 90329 behind the signal box. The line from Halifax to Queensbury was opened by the Halifax & Ovenden Joint Railway between 1874 and 1878 and was extended to Keighley in 1884. Despite being the first station to open, the construction of Halifax North Bridge probably caused the biggest headache. Firstly, massive slum clearances had to be undertaken to build a 400-yard viaduct from Halifax (Old) station. Then, the North Bridge carrying the main road into the town from Leeds and Bradford had to be demolished and rebuilt 11 ft higher to clear the tracks. Another viaduct had to be built north of the station to clear a culvert, and then the line ascended steeply through the Woodside tunnel, where a landslip delayed construction of the line northwards for twelve months. Freight services between North Bridge and Halifax's GN/L&Y joint station continued until April 1974 when the site was cleared for a supermarket, car park and leisure centre.
David J. Mitchell

Bibliography

Stephen Batty: *British Rail at Work –
West Yorkshire*; Ian Allan

Hugh Ballantyne: *The Colour of British Rail –
Vol 2 – West Coast Main Line*; Atlantic
Transport Publishers

Murray Brown: *Rail Portfolios – The Deltics*;
Ian Allan

A.K. Butlin: *Diesel Disposal*; Coorlea Publishing

A.N. Curtis: *Western Liveries*; A&C Services

A.N. Curtis: *Western Dawn*; A&C Services

H.G. Forsythe: *Men of the Diesels*; Atlantic
Transport Publishers

Brian Haresnape: *British Rail Fleet Survey –
Vols 1,2,3,4,7,8*; Ian Allan

Ken Hoole: *Trains in Trouble – Vol 3*; Atlantic
Transport Publishers

L.A. Nixon: *BR Colour Album*; Ian Allan

Robert Stephens: *Diesel Pioneers*; Atlantic
Transport Publishers

British Rail – Main Line Gradient Profiles;
Ian Allan

*British Railways Pre-Grouping Atlas and
Gazetteer*; Ian Allan

Diesel & Electric Loco Register;
Platform 5 Publishing

Other Publications: *Backtrack Magazine,
Modern Railways, Railway Magazine, Railway
World, Railway Observer, Traction Magazine,
Trains Illustrated, The World of Trains*

Published by Rails Publishing
www.capitaltransport.com

Printed by Parksons Graphics

© Derek Huntriss 2014
Designed by Derek Huntriss

Acknowledgements

Most railway photographers reserved their film
for recording the last workings of BR steam and
colour photographs of green diesels are scarce.
I am indebted to all those who contributed
irreplaceable transparencies and high resolution
scans for inclusion in this title. We all owe them
our sincere thanks for recording a period which
has become as remote as the steam age itself.
Special thanks are offered to David Postle at
the Kidderminster Railway Museum and Paul
Shackcloth of the Manchester Locomotive
Society in Stockport for access to archive
material.

Front Cover
The famous Connel Bridge across the Falls of Lora
was built to carry the Ballachulish branch of the
Caledonian Railway's Callander and Oban line across
Loch Etive. The tidal nature of the water and the
speed of the current meant that the bridge had to be
designed with its piers almost 'on shore'. Here
BRCW Type 2 Bo-Bo No D5352 is seen crossing the
bridge with freight from Ballachulish on 10 August
1962. *Neville Simms*

Title Page
This excellent picture shows brand new BR/Sulzer
Type 2 Bo-Bo No D7534 catching the sun as it peers
from the darkness of Nottingham (16A) mpd on 28
March 1965. *Bill Wright*

Rear Cover
English Electric Type 4 1Co-Co1 No D232 *Empress
of Canada* approaches Grayrigg with a Glasgow to
Euston express on 25 July 1963. *Peter Fitton*